Copyright 2020 - by Beth Costanzo

Whether you are visiting your local aquarium or going into the ocean for a snorkel adventure, there are many different sea creatures that you may encounter. Every marine animal, from the smallest fish to the largest whale, has a unique story to tell.

In this booklet, I want to discuss a fascinating sea creature that may seem terrifying at first. That creature is the **hammerhead shark**. **Hammerhead sharks** are known for their distinctive appearance. Most likely, you find them intimidating or even terrifying. But putting that aside, **hammerhead sharks** live an extremely fascinating life. Because of this, let's take a closer look.

THE HAMMERHEAD SHARK: A FASCINATING MARINE CREATURE

Like the other sea creatures that we've studied, let's start by examining the *hammerhead shark*'s appearance. Looking at the *hammerhead shark*, you can see that its head has a signature hammer shape (called a cephalofoil). It is flattened and laterally extended.

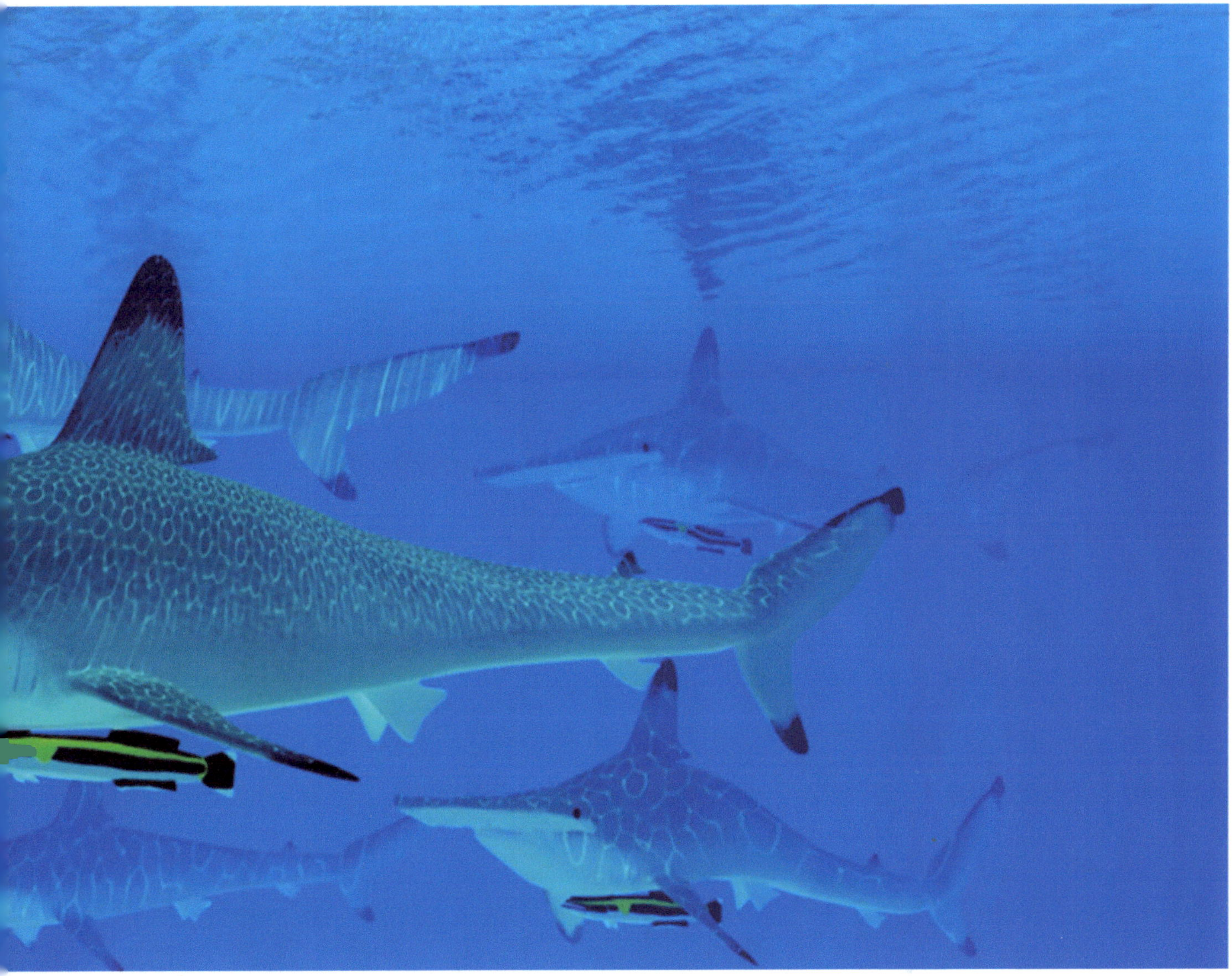

WWW.ADVENTURESOFSCUBAJACK.COM

Ultimately, their heads are distinctive and unusual. No other shark looks like them and one of the theories is that their heads have a hammer-like shape because it may have enhanced the *hammerhead shark*'s vision. The eyes of the hammerhead shark offer 360 degrees of vision on the vertical plane. What this means is that the *hammerhead shark*, at all times, can see above and below itself.

Along with the unique shape of their head, the known species of hammerhead sharks can be quite long. The shortest *hammerhead shark* is about three feet while the longest can be almost 20 feet. They can also be very heavy, weighing up to 1300 pounds. These sharks are big, so you'll want to steer clear if you are swimming next to them. Along with their large size and weight, *hammerhead sharks* have a light gray color and a green-colored tint. If you were to look at their bellies, you would see that their bellies are white. This isn't just because the white color looks good. *Hammerhead sharks*'s white bellies can help it blend into the ocean, allowing it to better approach prey from above

Map of Hammerhead Shark Habitat

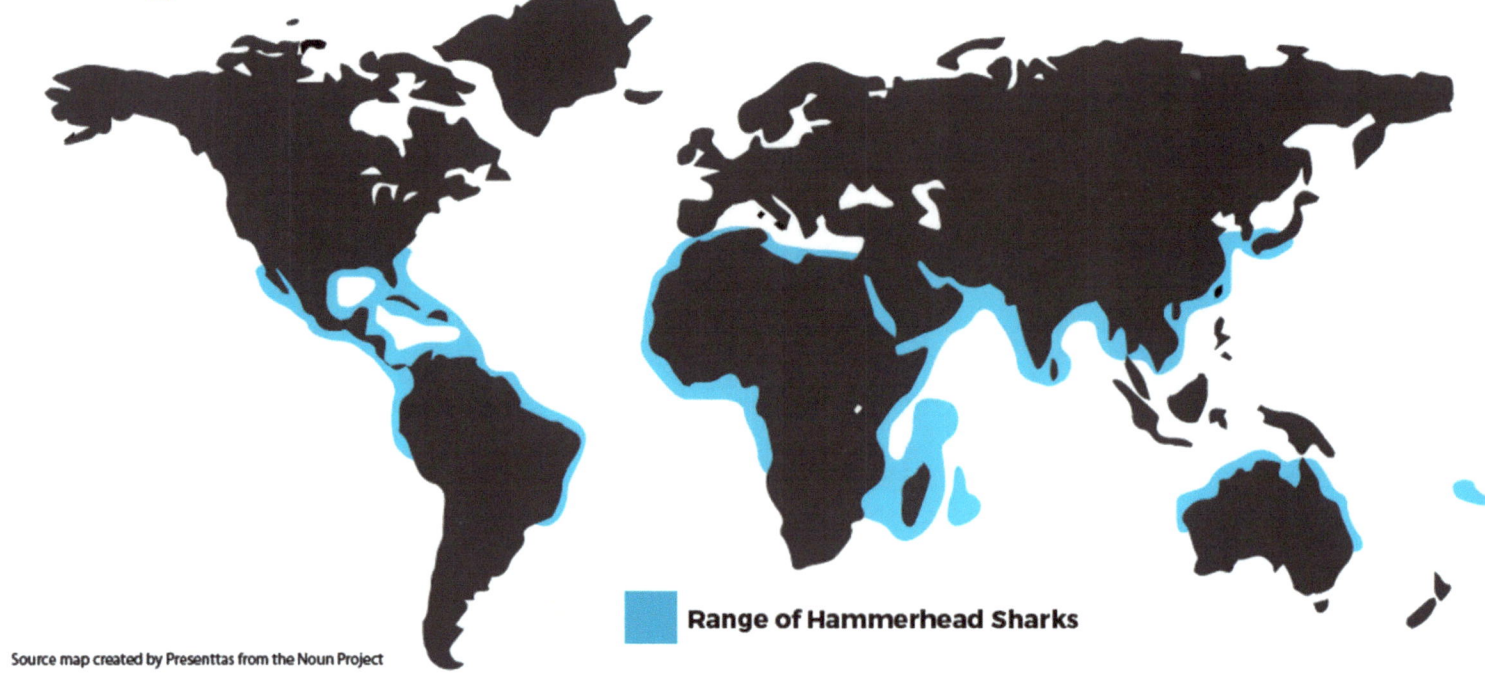

Range of Hammerhead Sharks

Source map created by Presenttas from the Noun Project

Beyond the appearance of the *hammerhead shark*, let's talk about where you can find them. *Hammerhead sharks* can be found near several countries. For example, *hammerhead sharks* have been seen near Colombia, the Galapagos Islands, Costa Rica, Hawaii, and eastern Africa. Most likely, you won't be seeing *hammerhead sharks* in the wild unless you go to one of these exotic locations. Even there, you will have to keep your eyes open to see them. Hammerhead sharks mostly swim with each other (specifically, in groups called schools) during the day and hunt by themselves at night.

There is a wide range of species of *hammerhead sharks*. Some of those species include the **scoophead**, the **winghead shark**, the **Carolina hammerhead**, and the **smooth hammerhead**. The **winghead shark**, **scalloped hammerhead**, and **great hammerhead** are considered endangered. The scalloped bonnethead is also considered near threatened. No matter the species, humans are working hard to prevent the hammerhead from going extinct.

WWW.ADVENTURESOFSCUBAJACK.COM

Hammerhead sharks tend to eat a wide range of food. Some of their prey includes squid, octopus, crustaceans, and other fish. However, *hammerhead sharks* are particularly attracted to stingrays. When *hammerhead sharks* go hunting, they swim along the bottom of the ocean. It uses its uniquely-shaped head to search for food. Once the *hammerhead shark* sees some prey, it will use its head as a secret weapon. For example, when the *hammerhead shark* is hunting down a stingray, it will pin down the stingray on the ocean floor, feeding on the stingray when it is startled and in shock.

WWW.ADVENTURESOFSCUBAJACK.COM

Along with fish, some *hammerhead sharks* tend to eat seagrass. Specifically, the **Bonnethead** *Hammerhead Shark* is known to eat seagrass, essentially making it an omnivore. An omnivore is an animal that eats both meat and plants. Also, one of the most interesting things about *hammerhead sharks* is that they will actually eat other *hammerhead sharks*, including their own young. The specific species that engages in cannibalism is the great hammerhead shark. Among other *hammerhead sharks*, however, this is quite rare.

WWW.ADVENTURESOFSCUBAJACK.COM

Like many sharks, you may be wondering whether they are dangerous to humans. You can rest easy with *hammerhead sharks*. Since the year 1580, there have been 17 documented *hammerhead shark* attacks against humans. Those attacks have been unprovoked by the sharks, meaning that they didn't start them. Out of those 17 attacks, not one human has died.

In fact, the *hammerhead shark* has more to fear from us than we have to fear from them. This is because *hammerhead sharks* are sometimes hunted by humans. In some Asian countries (particularly China), *hammerhead sharks* are hunted for their fins. Those fins are then used in delicacies like shark fin soup.

In other cultures, however, *hammerhead sharks* are honored and praised. One great example comes from Hawaii. In Hawaiian culture, sharks are considered to be gods of the sea. They protect humans and clear the oceans of excessive life. Some even believe that *hammerhead sharks* are reincarnated, meaning that dead humans have come back to life and taken the form of sharks

MORE FUN FACTS ABOUT HAMMERHEAD SHARKS

As you can tell, the *hammerhead shark* is one of the most fascinating creatures in our oceans. Here are some more fun facts about the *hammerhead shark*.

WWW.ADVENTURESOFSCUBAJACK.COM

1 If you see a hammerhead shark in an aquarium, it will likely be the Bonnethead Shark. This is because of its smaller size compared to other hammerheads.

2 The hammerhead shark has some pores on its head, which can help it detect electricity from other living creatures.

3 Few aquariums can keep hammerhead sharks for long periods due to their need for very large and special tanks.

4 Hammerhead sharks live between 20 and 30 years.

WWW.ADVENTURESOFSCUBAJACK.COM

A pregnant female hammerhead shark can carry her eggs for about 8 to 10 months. **5**

6 The hammerhead shark is often found in temperate and tropical waters.

In the summer, hammerhead sharks are seen migrating to colder waters. **7**

8 Hammerhead sharks have an extra-tall dorsal fin. This makes them easy to see.

HAMMERHEAD SHARK ACTIVITIES

Let's have fun with some actitivites of the Hammerhead Sharks!

TRACING

Trace the word below

Hammerhead shark

COUNTING

Count the hammerhead sharks then circle the correct answer

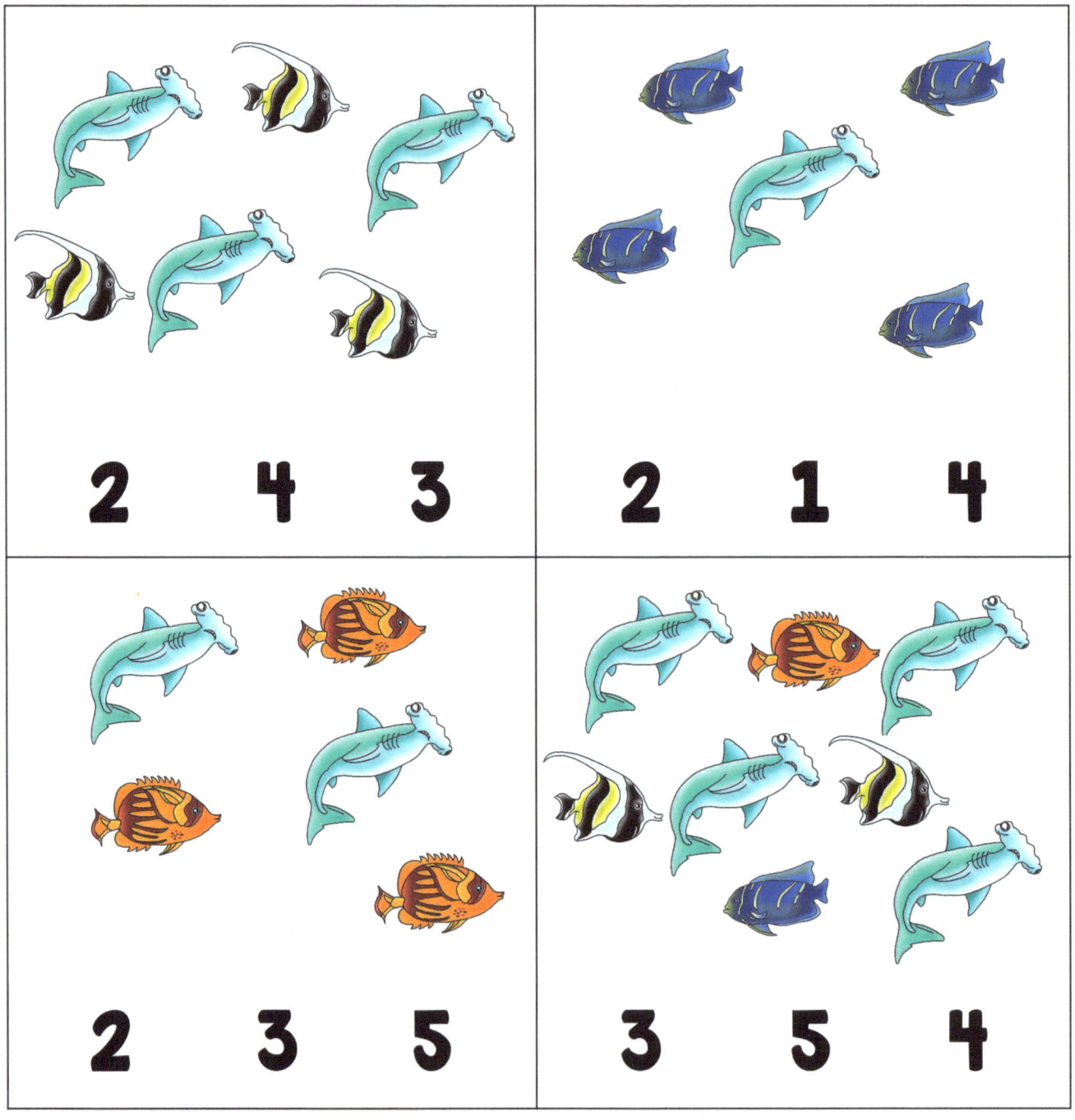

DOT TO DOT

Match the dots to finish the drawing

COLORING

Color the hammerhead shark below

VISIT US AT
WWW.ADVENTURESOFSCUBAJACK.COM

www.ingramcontent.com/pod-product-compliance
Lightning Source LLC
Chambersburg PA
CBHW041439010526
44118CB00002B/122